Landscape of a Woman and a Hummingbird

Also by Joseph Milosch
The Lost Pilgrimage Poems, Poetic Matrix Press

Landscape of a Woman and a Hummingbird

Joseph Milosch

Poetic Matrix Press

Cover art and cover design by Molly Weller,
author *Finding Passages*, Poetic Matrix Press

copyright © 2014 by Joseph Milosch

ISBN: 978-0-9860600-3-8

All rights reserved. No part of this book may be used or reproduced in any manner whatsoever without written permission, except in the case of quotes for personal use and brief quotations embedded in critical articles or reviews.

Poetic Matrix Press
www.poeticmatrix.com

Acknowledgements

Thanks to the following publications where these poems first appeared:

CPITS Anthology
In the Deep End
Magee Park Poets Anthology
Manzanita Anthology
Poems and Plays
Poetic Matrix Press
Redwood Coast Review
Roads Poetry
San Diego Poetry Annual
San Diego Writer's Monthly
San Gabriel Valley Poetry Calendar
Short Poem/ Getting Published
TidePools Anthology
Write Room

My thanks also to my wife, Patsy and friends James Arthur, Glover Davis, minerva, & Georgette James for their critiques of my poems. I would like to thank Sandra Alcosser for her enthuiastic support.

Contents

Acknowledgements / v
Contents / vi
Dedication / ix

Landscape of a Woman and a Hummingbird / 3
Yellowstone Meditation # 3 / 4
   Yellowstone Lake
In the Beijing Bell Temple / 5
Climbing Modjeska Peak / 6
Workday before Christmas / 7
Under the Worn Cap / 9
Yellowstone Buffalo / 11
Landscape of Seals on the Beach / 12
At My Brother's Stone / 13
The Wish to Begin / 15
The Walker / 16
The Red & the Black / 17
Summer Night / 22
To Mount St. Helens, Erupting / 24
Near the Old Western Town & Museum, / 25
   Sundance's Grave Stood on a Knoll beside the Town
Women of the Time between Night / 27
   and the Morning Star
Great Grandfather and the Compost Pile / 28
The Moon Canyon Fire / 29
Yellowstone Meditation # 1 / 30
   on the Planets: Neptune & Mars
Below Zero Days / 32
Soup Bowls / 33
Working Yarn / 34
Landscape of a Childhood / 36
Father of Boards and Woodwinds / 37

Bottle Fire / 38
Rutting Bulls in Yellowstone / 42
Locating the Pacific Crest Trail / 43
The Gust of Wind / 45
Friday's Fish Supper / 47
The Soft Tug of the Tongue and Lips / 48
Awakening / 49
A Blizzard Drove / 51
During a Family Reunion / 52
Landscape: Great Grandfather and Walnut Tree / 53
The Afternoon of Good and Plenty / 54
Blue Stool / 56
Kings River Canyon / 57
Meditation on An Uplifted Beach / 58
Yellowstone Meditation #4 / 62
   Sunday School
Bell Ringer / 63
Landscape of a Young Woman and a Pool / 64
Below the Feet of Orion — Huanusco, Mexico / 65

Author Biography
Press Producers

Dedication

These poems are dedicated to my wife, Patsy.

Landscape of a Woman and a Hummingbird

Landscape of a Woman and a Hummingbird

He twists his neck to catch the sun,
which turns his throat to the same shade
of red as the fluid in the gourd-shaped feeder.

Peeling grilled tomatoes, she lifts her head
to see him dip his beak, turn his head,
and burst into shadow.

As they slip through her fingers, tomato seeds
become prayer beads, which seem suspended
for a moment before falling into her salsa.

Yellowstone Meditation #3
Yellowstone Lake

Fishing, a bald eagle abandons the updraft.
Diving, he extends his claws into the lake

and climbs, clutching a rainbow, which dribbles
droplets into the mirror-like surface.

I am a shadow on the roadside and become a shine
of darkness when I dance steps that release me

as magically as a fish dropped from talons.
Twirling, I re-enter my life with an open mouth.

In the Beijing Bell Temple

"Knowledge does not require a belief in heaven or hell, or a labyrinth of philosophy to exist." — C. Milosz

I

Behind the counter of miniature bells,
the slim caretaker smiles, and believing
the temple empty, she plays a melody
so sweet the birds gather in elliptic circles
to hear her mallet strike softly the bells.
I sit out of sight as the tune she phrases
employs brass and wood to conjure
the Northern lights. "Fish," Grandpa said,
"Some we toss back and others we eat."
In Beijing I wonder how a mechanic
with a third grade education paraphrased
Marcus Aurelius. As I listen to her,
my thoughts becomes as elusive as the glimpse
of a fish surfacing between boat and shallows.

II

Rocking in my patio chair, I listen to chimes
and return to the slender musician in her
olive dress. Her bell song reminded me
of an island where sunrise acts as a bugle call
for mosquitoes to swarm above the rabbit's carcass.
During the day, sound dies at the drip line
of a cluster of beech trees. At sunset sound gains
strength enough to release the echoes of a woodpecker,
to uncloak frogs along the shore, and allow fish
to splash in search of game. All this appears normal
to the fishermen, watching the aurora borealis.

Climbing Modjeska Peak

It is the same, climbing a mountain
or a high-tension power pole.
The world becomes smaller
as I climb, fixing my eyes
on fractures and fissures
no thicker than a quarter inch.
Creeping up, I follow a trail
of finger-holds as I scale
rock faces, not metal struts.

The world is above, below,
and around me, but I
can't see more than
a foot in front of me.
Pausing on a ledge, I repeat
a cliché about the view.
At the top, the world expands
into a giant circle.

Standing in the center,
I stretch my arms
and become a cross
visible from the coast;
continuing to lift my arms,
I form a Y. Spinning once
around, I find the world
stands still, and that the earth
shrinks to the size of a pedestal
to keep me from falling into space.

Workday before Christmas

Torrey pines
buckwheat,
black sage,
and beside a granite boulder
deer tracks,
a coyote's nose
sniffing,
rubbed in dirt,
licked.

Descending slopes,
a wind-blown cloud
coats windows,
exhaust stacks,
and the dozer's
vinyl seats.
With hammer—punch
I remove the ripper's pin
as sweat,
fog,
dirt,
later
rain
mingles
along my arms.

Driving home in darkness,
I undress
in the work shed.
Scraping mud
off my boots,
I bang it off my socks,

and run into the kitchen,
wearing jacket,
shorts,
sandals.
Smell tamale makings
chile, masa,
garlic, pork,
as Patsy's fingers,
caked
in dough,
are cool
on my thighs.

Under the Worn Cap

To work, one must accept pain,
which rides the bronco-like
back of your hammer
and appears as bloody,
finger prints on a rag.

Even though he's bored
with your tales about
the cracked hands
of your ancestors,
he listens to your stories.

As he accompanies you at work,
he slips a pebble of hot slag
into your boot, spills aspirin
in your truck, and redirects
the sledge into your shin.

When you think he's disappeared
in the dirt fields, blossoming
with clay-clumped windrows,
he appears as a coiled-stinger
shadow under a pile of pipes.

You see his silhouette
gliding across the job
and identify him
by his missing feathers
and the sun shinning
through the slats of his wings.

He visits you on Sunday
after you worked six
twelve hour shifts.
He finds you with your hands
curled around a cup
while you stare at the moon slice,
floating above the shallow horizon.

You know him
by the rolled cuffs of his shirt —
by the smear of grease on his cheek—
by the Irish jig he dances
under the worn cap of your knee.

Yellowstone Buffalo

Jumping a log, a young bull stumbles over a berm
before attempting to mount a cow.
Four bulls run to bellow him off her rump.
Forming a circle, they face each other.
The first bellow is silenced by the second,
which is silenced by a third as birds
walk below the bulls' beards.

In this premature rut, the younger bulls
lower their heads, and one by one drag
their tails like loose ends of rope.
The remaining two bellow, paw, and lunge.
The winner shakes his head, bellows, and
between bellows, he lolls his tongue.

The loser turns to eye the tourist traffic.
He rams a bronze Bronco. He rams it again —
double quick. Then, he shakes his head
as if to forget defeat. Behind him,
geese descend into the river. Cupping wings,
they lower their heads and extend their feet.

Above their splash-landing, an osprey glides
beneath the milling clouds, and the quickly
darkening meadow drives the herd to circle,
bumping rumps and sides. When lightning strikes,
the swift and secret force of the land startles us.
As thunder echoes, the tourist, buffalo, and
geese direct their eyes to the North where
merging currents of air spring into wind.

Landscape of Seals on the Beach

Grey Island on the Eastern Frontier
of the Tasman Sea, your beaches littered
with rocks, rolling out of waves —
driftwood, wrought with sea weed –
and yawns of seal cows, waking in late afternoon.

It must have been a fine day when the fog dissipated,
revealing your seal cows for the first time.
Appearing as thick logs of mahogany, they stretched
and scratched themselves with their flippers.

I watch your cows. Some sleep as others ignore the cloud
full of rain that shadows the beach. Waiting for the hoarse
bellows to announce the arrival of bulls, the herd becomes
startled by the commotion of seabirds flying from their roost.

At My Brother's Stone

My brother and I
walked southwest
through cut cornstalks
in Burkett's field.
We crossed Spruce Creek
and broke crusted mud
into a slender path.
Hunting mice, squirrels, each other,
we paused beside the patch of cattails
and looked at the beaver's hut,
at dogs tracks along the lake's edge.
Bending, John ran his hand
down the fallen maple branch
frozen to the shore.

He removed a leaf
and laid it in his palm
to protect its ice plating.
Lifting the leaf,
John slid it between the sun
and his face until
leaf finger shadows
striped his nose.
Outside the trees, wind turned cold,
and a bundle of crescent shaped icicles
hardened at the hut's base.

Here I look at his stone
broken by the letters of his name,
by his life dates,
and in the middle
of a wide cross

the slice of a brown curled leaf.
Closing my eyes,
I see John standing
with a feather strung
to his coat's zipper.
His thumb rubs
the wood point of his spear
as he watches an owl glide,
beak down
under birch limbs.

The Wish to Begin

Burnt branches of maple mark the wooden rails,
as moonlight crosses the porch to circle
the plastic daisies, pasted to a window.

As it scorched my parent's graves, the wild fire
forgot its voice, and seed burrs of woodland grasses
fell from its ancient leggings.

Why wish to be five again?
When the house became full
of moonlight and shadows,
love descended from the one in the night gown.

Leaning on the upstairs rail, she watched
as I raised my hand to her.
In return she lifted her hand until it became lost
in the darkness above her.

An orphan at forty isn't as sad
as an orphan at five, yet
memories are less vivid than dreams.

A shaft of moonlight exposes
a spider colonizing
the barren landscape of the fireplace.

Now, the wish to begin again
ascends as the warm breeze
of an Indian summer
crossing the Huron.

The Walker

I haven't worked for 24 weeks.
Instead, I walk the streets
in the hours I used to drive.

During these months,
I've come to wonder
if I'm too old to work.

Pausing outside a small shop beside
an equipment yard, I watch a mechanic
begin to torque the engine bolts.

The shop employs a Doberman Pincher
for a security guard. Startled by a black bird
jumping the curb, I look into the gutter and

see a baseball beside a cat-eyed marble.
I grab the ball and roll it across my hand.
From the stiches, I clean moss, mud,

and wonder if our commonality,
the ball's and mine, is that nothing
is more useless than we are

unless it is the sycamore leaves,
which have remained long enough
to coat the concrete black.

The Red & the Black

I

Olive-skinned under bar lights,
a woman stands straightening her red shorts.
She removes black glass earrings,
shows them to me,
saying, 'Apache tears from Utah.'
She places them on a napkin,
turns them into the light.
'My ex gave them to me, naturally
shaped like tears.' Picking one up
by its gold wire, she blows on it,
polishes it, and slides it into her ear.
Closing her eyes, she clips it, smiles.
'He was into black,
he had this dog, "a Samoan,"
black except for an orange patch
on his cheek. Named him Flame.'
Opening her wallet, she flips to her man's picture.
'Here he is in Chicago.'

I see
Nazi
insignias
on the chest
and arm
of his leather jacket.

II

Leaving the bar, we enter the alley.
Fred went to Chicago, said
it was a march that would push

concert reviews and baseball scores
out of the papers.
Leaning against the white wall
of her back apartment,
I pull her to me. A door slams.
She leads me
under bronze
flakes of flame,
chained to the candle chime
on her porch light.
We pass through her doorway,
and with a thrust of my jaw
I acknowledge her collage
       (The Nazi Flag;
       The U.S. Flag;
       Hitler's picture;
       The U.S. Confederate Flag.)
A letter lies
beside the lamp
on a black cloth iron cross.
I think
of some other night
she had stood here with her lover.
My bike
modified
reminds her of him,
of the ride to Texas.
She likes Naked Poetry
written in orange
across the side
of my dark blue tank.
She talks of the union
of body and machine,
of frosted air
running up her sleeves
across her breasts,

and in his hometown
she wore his jacket.
I put these things aside
in her room smelling of musk,
lighted by a candle on her clock radio.
She adjusts peacock feathers in a vase,
brushes wrinkles from the blouse
folded over her wicker chair,
and turns to me
a silver bird on her wrist.

III

On her arm
I trace
flakes of flame
of a cat's face
with a necklace
around its neck.
'I hated my dad,'
she said, and talks
of how her mother
dislikes Fred.
"Your father
fought against
his type in Europe.
And what do you do?
You live with dirt!"
Her mother
doesn't want to hear
about the Jews
or Hitler's conquest.
She knows only
what her husband tells her.

This pierced-
eared woman
reaches out
as if I were Fred.
She wants me
to force her
to surrender
to the blue, black,
cool of metal,
the chrome, and steel current
flowing inside me.
I am close enough
to bruise the rose tattoo
on her inside thigh.
Close enough to see
the crescent scar
under her lip,
to feel there is
something
in her unclasped hair
in her hands, and mouth.

IV

I look at Fred's skull ring
hanging from her chain.
I think
of the chain
locking the door
of my garage,
and the times
I have stepped
among the wood,
the concrete,
the tools hung

on two by fours.
From there
I wiped rain
off my bike,
and watched
the black neighbor's daughter
moon walk.
She did her outside dance
between shade
of palm and elm.
From there
I listened
to the oriental owners
of the corner store,
understanding only
round nickel tones
of their talk.
In my garage
I heard
a sound
like rust flakes
shaken in a can.
Though
there is nothing
except
rain swollen studs,
cobwebs.
I saw Juan run
with his little brother
down the alley
jumping
puddle to puddle.

Summer Night

I leave my wife behind cream paper shades
and lean against the rail into the wind.
The fog appears as water beads on wire
fence posts, my cotton shirt. I wipe my beard.
I look at clouds, light poles, a stalking cat.
Three walkways down I watch a chained pit bull
snapping at men attacking it. "Home Boy!"
Len yells throwing a broom under his dog,
it skips spear-like then glances off legs, ribs
and rolls with dog and chain in dirt, leaves, dust.
He's a soiled force, whose voice is like the rasp
of rusty chimes knocking in wind. I've heard
Len growl and rage like mad. He said, "Some nights
I wake and feel I've worked up a good sweat,
and the wind comes, hitting me in the back
like dad, who thought he'd control me. He would
belt me from behind when he had the urge."
Len dreams he hears steel ropes vibrate across
the echoes of his spirit's split-bone howl.
Here birds group on the branches swaying north,
as my wife sleeps in her buttonless gown.
Embroidered tulips cover her right breast,
white orchids cross her shoulder, her silk
collar wrinkles under a curling hair.
The police stop in broken rings of dust,
waking the remaining sleepers on this street.
I turn to find my wife in the doorway.
Her robe rests on the knuckles of her toes.
I open the screen and we withdraw to sit
and talk of moving north. She remembers home,
her childhood in Tulare, the work in fields.

She helped her mother pick tomatoes, grapes.
She made tortillas, or lunch, or changed diapers
as aunts and cousins filled the rooms with talk,
or jokes, or songs as light as birds. Outside
our door loud cries, "Let Go! Let Go!" as flesh
is squeezed between car hoods and clubs. Tonight
she won't talk of arms scratched by cotton's thorns,
the dirt silting across her lip, her bra,
the ugly smell of diesel, coffee, fruit.
She flinches, thinking about the lead man's look,
her mother's brow furrowed in the sun's ruins,
and once wiping her hat's sweat pad, she had
a vision of her daughters picking crops.

To Mount St. Helens, Erupting

Spinning the woodland
   into clouds of burls and soil,
your rhythm drums,

and your wave beats the air
   with amber tongues.
Go ahead, blow mud, pluck trees.

Melting jewels thump low and add
   a backbeat like tubas in the
ensemble of ice and dirt.

When soil begins to shift into movement,
   strings of boiling sap stream
from conifers and broadleaf trees.

Instantly, your mountainside bursts
   into flame, and slopes slide in a fluid
motion like an orchestra's string section.

As your crescendo entwines cinders
   with sky and hissing steam,
your lava glows like molten metal.

After residue settles like snow
   and silence echoes silence,
one sees that grass won't grow
   while so infused with ash.

Near the Old Western Town & Museum, Sundance's Grave Stood on a Knoll beside the Town

  Above the mountain peaks, sparse clouds
appeared in midmorning. As noon cut short
the shadows of rails and posts, the town dressed
in the color of dust on sky.
  Standing under the porch awning,
I rubbed the rail and watched tourists fill the cabin.
They shuffled across the hideout's floor
as if indifferent to historic places
of mythic escapes.
  The table with its deck of cards
seemed out of place. Who leaned the chair
against the wall? West of the cabin stood
a corral and beside it a dirt road, leading
to the town's boot hill.
  Tumbleweed grew around his grave, covered
with napkins, cardboard trays, and a crumpled cup.
Beside me stood a man in a black cap with white
letters, NRA. He shined his tin buckle, imprinted with a horn.
"Here's the grave of a great outlaw," he said to his son.
  Stooping, I touched the ground before arranging
pea sized gravel into a ring. Hollowing out the center,
I broke old twigs and created a toy campfire.
As a boy, I dreamed of an outlaw life with its night
of clouds circling below the moon.
  I dreamed of howls, wind in rocks, and my horse
pulling against his tether. I dreamed of money, women, and
saloons full of cigars and beer. I dreamed of how it had to end
with me roped to an Ox-bow-shaped tree as I sat upon my horse.

  Now as I kneel and rub the soil from my fingertips,
I find I no longer shade that dream with the color

of a cougar's fur, or look into Sundance's life
as if it contained a map with an X.
    What remains is the smell of dried weeds
and the cold wind, dropping from the Rockies.

Women of the Time between Night and the Morning Star

On this morning in the last years of the Twentieth Century,
it is near dawn. The night is so clear I imagine myself
to be a wagon master 300 years ago on his way tell this story
to the minister-slash-magistrate.

On my drive to work at the Lagoon mitigation, the moon orbits
closer than it will for another 300 years, and I see three pelicans
glide like a line of witches threading the horizon. Women of fish
and waves to what do your sticks point?

Before sunrise, I arrive on site to find my work crumpled
along the shore. What am I to think, seeing the three of you cross
the moon's face for the third time? In your low orbit did you see
the sand cliff collapse to expose the ancient child?

Her skeleton hands curled in sleep, and a shell bracelet
encompassing her wrist. How did a bird's skull come
to rest against her knees? Who placed those charcoal squares
below her ribs? Are the answers found in the roots of a sea rose?

Woman of the time between night and the Morning Star,
is it because the moon is as close as it will be for another
three centuries that the land vibrates like a drumskin?
Now, my heart's shadows forms an image of an image

of a man, walking in the work boots of his life. Nevertheless,
three people are silent inside me. The man I am, the man
I want to be, and the child, who a centuries old flood buried,
carried, and planted in this lagoon.

As I raise my flashlight to see her, my arm's silhouette moves
to meet her. I see my shirt cuff's shadow touch her as gently
as the sea breeze blows my hair across my forehead. As I turn
to look westward, the moon touches the edge of ocean and sky.

Great Grandfather and the Compost Pile

Light clouds appeared along the upper edge
of that photo of winter wheat and snow.
Shadows hid below shadows as he worked
the compost with a pitchfork.

Standing out of range of the lens, I became
mesmerized by his unhurried strokes.
Lifting his fork, he turned it so that
the mulch fell like feed from a scoop.

Frozen in mid flap, his shirt-tail exposed his rump
where crickets, moths, and ants were attached
by a web. After taking the picture, grandma laughed
and promised to show it during the holidays.

In those days he sat at the head of the table and chewed
the end of his cigar. I sat on his lap as he mumbled
what could have been lyrics to a peasant song, and
unintelligible as they were, I knew them as the words

a man passes to his offspring. He wanted me to know
how to hand-milk cows, or how to mend harnesses,
or shoe a horse. This was his gift, as unknowable
as the pastures and barns of his homeland.

Above the pile his pitchfork swept through egg shells
and corn husks. As I watched him, we shared our breath
with the incoming blizzard.

The Moon Canyon Fire

All night the head lamps attached to our hardhats bobbed
as we worked the fire line. The five-gallon water bags
on our backs grew lighter as we sprayed embers
before the coldest part of morning came.

As the moon began to sink, Nancy came over. Squatting,
she took off her hard hat and laid it upside-down in front of her.
Pulling off her blue bandana, she rubbed the sides of her head,
by moving her hands as fast as she could.

Squatting next to her, I pulled a package of instant coffee
from my pocket. Taking it, she placed it on her thigh,
and separated the grains into two equal parts by rubbing
her finger across the crinkled sack.

Tearing the packet in two, she handed me one
to place between my cheek and gum. Lifting our
tool's handles, we leaned on them as we watched
daylight bring color to the smoky hillsides.

I think now of things I could've have said or gestures I might
have made to develop the moment into intimacy. I mean….
As her teeth touched her lower lip, the sun appeared.
The stars and moon remained visible. We saw our breath.

Instead, I remained beside her. We leaned on our tools,
pushed our hardhats closer together by working them
with the tool's blade. Looking at the hills, we beheld the order
of fire with its distant flames and layers of smoke and fiery ash.

Gazing on its calamity—charred oaks below the greasewood
skeletons, the lone chimney picketed by burned ruins—
we caught each other's eyes before an updraft of the ocean's air
created steam with the coals surrounding us.

Yellowstone Meditation #1
On the Planets: Neptune & Mars

Cody Campground has several log cabins, equipped
with a porch swing, a Dutch door, and log latch.
After unpacking, my wife heads for the showers,
and as I wait for her, I brew coffee before I swing
and read 'Cosmos' by Carl Sagan.

As the sky darkens, I see first the rim of the horizon
then more stars appear in groups or as a single point.
Neptune is beyond sight, but near the Morning Star,
I see red when Mars appears shortly before
the appearance of Orion's sword.

As the camp becomes quiet, I'm embarrassed
to swing because of the squeak of chain on hook.
As I quit rocking, crickets sing louder. In the desert
the night sky is clear of clouds, but in these mountains,
clouds move between the planets and me.

Before Venus emerges, the moon appears,
casting cloud shadows over the mountain peaks.
Owls screech but their voices carry no remnants
of ancient warriors or soldiers. During Vietnam,
some of the war dissenters were fond of saying

that the Romans honored the gods of the dead and war
before going to war while we honor the God of peace
by going to war. The easy response might contains
elements of irony or tragedy, but that's too academic.
When surrounded by voices of crickets and owls —

clouds and stars, one does not forget their war or
the ancient gods, who are far away as the planets

whose namesakes carry the trident and the sword.
Storms and war rage tonight as over the radio,
NASA reports that the earth and moon stand still daily

for 3.9 seconds; then, perception transforms: changing
here in the vast silence of the campground as well as
in the vastness of space — where the planet of the King
of the lower world orbits out of sight, and Mars blinks red
in the lower reaches of the sky.

Below Zero Days

With an unzipped jacket
and sweat dripping
from my hair, I walked
on crusted snow
through islands and woods.

The branches of an uprooted pine
formed a windbreak
like a muskrat's hut.
I could sit for hours
with my .22
behind a wall of woven
limb and snow. I shot
this log, that stump,
or a clump of snow-
covered grasses
the wind shaped
into a rabbit or wolverine.

On those winter afternoons
the cold moved slow
as if afraid of the trees,
dropping icicles
as if to mark there presence.
I wondered
what it would be like
to grow old or cold
as I fired my weapon,
which made an axe
chopping sound.

Soup Bowls
—For Bobbie Roberts

Pot stickers
stuffed mushrooms
soup bowls steaming
on a glass table

No one wants to leave
this place of lemon walls
and wicker chairs
where we share
our thoughts around
the lip of the room

Working Yarn

What falls and what perishes: the plum
        colored scarf –the blue gloves – the sweater,
              frayed at the cuffs.

When Edna knitted, she rocked, whispering to herself.
        Often she spoke the oldest mystery first.
              Over and under…one. Over and under…two,
            and then came three.

Sometimes she thought she heard something
        like a highlander's flute or shivered
              as if touched by the air preceding a gale.

After a half a century, her work was everywhere:
        the school bus, cabinets, pews,
            and the priest's Plymouth.

Newborns wore her shawls. She worked the yarn.
        People shopped wearing her sweaters. She worked
            the yarn. Everyone who wore her gifts became
                a part of her past.

Upon seeing her work, she recalled her neighbor's lives:
        baptisms, first communions, funerals. These were
            her reasons for saying the town's history was
    her own.

Her work claimed nothing. It became lost
in snow drifts, cedar chests, or tossed
            in the cloak room of St. Jill's.

When she died, it was not
        surprising to find a ball of yarn
                beside her bible, which rested on a doily,
                        designed with a white Jesse tree.

No one bothered to open the book
        or remove the needles, marking
                perhaps, the last passage she might have read.

Landscape of a Childhood

I could've stayed home
like my more industrious
brothers, Mike and John.

One learned to cut wood
in a straight line; the other
learned piano scales.

I could have stayed home
and studied geography or
Robinson Crusoe.

Perhaps, it was my mother's
fault for calling me
her Rip Van Winkle.

In late autumn, I cut across
corn fields to trees, screening
the edges of a beaver pond;

eventually, I found a stump
and sat to watch the snow fall
as I smelled the last of autumn.

Father of Boards and Woodwinds

You walk through my bedroom.
The hair on your chest is the almond
color of your youth. You notice me
looking at you, and turn to look out
my window at the chain link fence,
screened with bare grape vines.

Traveling woods of knobbed twigs, you've
come from your grave, arriving with
the symmetry of a man. Your hair is combed
back, and your eyebrows are thin lines of hair.
You angle your head like a clarinetist,
listening for the echo bouncing off the wall.

I face you. Your hand holds a two by four,
the other cuts it with a skill saw. I demand
we speak to one another; we sit in a bar and
tell each other how the pain in our knees is real.
I demand we talk about holding a job while
we work to keep tone in our clarinets.

When we worked together, you said,
'Place the blade's width in your measurement.'
Sometimes I'd pay in silence the price of a bad cut:
a slap to the head or shoulder joint, then you'd
turn away, surrender to your woodwind,
and trim your breath into flat and sharp shades.

Your hands' shadows are gnarled, scarred roots
slanting towards the carpet. I don't want to be
the horn cradled in your hands, the door planed
to fit the jamb, but there is little time to talk
for the holes between worlds evaporate with
the night, and I'm alone, a template cut from flesh.

Bottle Fire
"When you can no longer work like a young man, they'll can you. Go to college. Otherwise you will end up poor and crippled like Butch." — Aunt Joan

Nothing could suppress her bitterness when her husband received a fifteen-dollar gift certificate for not missing a day of work in ten years. In front of everyone, Butch stood slopping beer as he shook his boss's hand. Then in that half holler voice that a drunk uses, he said, "I owe this to my wife! She tells me, I married you for better or worse not breakfast or lunch."

Her blood ran up her chin under her rouge, coloring her cheeks raw and open. She turned her head to avoid his breath that swarmed over her like ants. "Don't spend this in one place," he said, and she stood stiff as a board, resisting his hugs, his kisses. Butch ignored it all, acting as if she were having fun. Further back than the wall, I sat on a box in the coat room, and drank the beer Butch stashed for me.

During the funeral, I listened to the priest and thought about Aunt Joan. How hard she tried not to express her anger at the Christmas party before my induction. When she puckered her lips, the thin traces of her moustache would quiver mouse-like. Unable to contain herself, she tried to wedge herself between Butch and the new man's wife. I recalled the glint of gold in the light as well as the ruby stone in his pinkie ring. Quickly, he placed his hand on Joan's hip. He pushed her to the front and introduced her as his wife. About himself, he said, "I'm the company's kissing cousin." It seemed like fun to me.

After his funeral I drove to Lake Huron's shore to get drunk in his memory. I found a campground, built a fire, and listened to the waves coming ashore. Butch, I thought of your boyhood friend Bob. Sometimes he sat home for days not drinking, nor talking, nor eating. Nothing shook his focus on being lost, rifle-less, and floating over the German occupied Italian slopes. Butch, you saved his job, gave him money, or food, and twice paid his rent. Calling his spells, 'German Malaria,' you opened a bottle of whiskey. The two of you would drink, cry, and hug each other. You said to him, "I'll break Hitler's nose when I see him in hell!"

On your deathbed you sank into the yellow lines of your face, and your eyes became two lakes iced over and seen from 2,000 feet high. Alone in the campground, I tasted ice in the lake's air. I tasted the sourness of death, and I promised you that I wouldn't let your memory fade like birch bark in the night's fog.

Before my Army induction, we camped at Clear Lake. Snow fell as I held the spool, and you reeled the line. You spoke to me as if I were your friend. "I thought after we kicked the Kraut's ass I'd come home and women would fall at my feet. I didn't know, didn't know." Dumping my coffee you gave me a shot of bourbon. Later by the campfire, we watched ashes float, and you talked of parachuting in Europe during WW II.

Wrapped in the aftertaste of your funeral, I left the warmth of the fire to walk along the shore of the lake. I pictured chutes white against black. They floated like food in a fish bowl. You felt at any moment you could be caught and filleted. You believed it was luck or God, who protected you.

When I was eight, you took me to a Union picnic; Joan wanted you to stop drinking. You grabbed a beer and took me canoeing. Somehow, we capsized in the Huron River.

You caught the root, as you held me from the current's grasp. After dragging us ashore, you put your arm across my shoulders. As we sat on the bank, a warm pit grew in our stomachs. You said defeating the currents and cheating death felt more satisfying than a slug of whiskey. As you rubbed my head, you told me WW II was the most thrilling time of your life, and you came back believing the only thing that mattered was the bond between fighting men.

When I became a veteran, you took me camping. Getting up for a refill you gave me your hand, pulled me from my chair. "Let's drink," you said, and your toast will forever ride the smoke that settled between the brush and water, between the trees, between our chests as we hugged. Now on the lake shore, I toe the water. I tell you that I've come to believe Joan was right when she said that drink allowed you to touch another.

Back at camp, I extinguish the fire. How you would fly off if anyone put a can or a bottle in the fire when we burned trash before breaking camp. "I almost lost my life for this country, I'll be damned if I'll let anyone trash it." Now in the campground on the lake, I flip through the events of your funeral. Aunt Joan asked me, "He was a good man, wasn't he?"

Butch, I know it is a sad game I'm playing, pretending you can listen, or that your drunkenness matters anymore. Your funeral day was a February day. The kind of day a man needed a warmer upper. A clump of snow melted under the pew, and on the way home from the graveyard, your son passed the bottle and said if it wasn't for me, there wouldn't have been enough pallbearers. I told him I owed you my friendship. You made sure I came to your Christmas parties. I remember the coat room, beer cached behind perfumed coats, tobacco smoke drifting in from the dance floor. Your voice would catch my ear like a bottle cracking in a campfire.

I knew something was going to happen. I thought how you applied heat to the party. I thought all the time I spent with you reshaped me like a bottle bowed and twisted under fire. I ignored your drunkenness. I ignored Joan's bitterness. What did I know?

The morning after the last Christmas party, I walked through brittle marsh reeds and across the lake to an island where a crescent of pines grew on the shore. There we met, broke ice, fished, and watched the sun glance off snow drifts, pails, and the iced stripes of the perch tossed onto a drift.

Rutting Bulls in Yellowstone

An eagle lands on top of a burnt
and branchless pine. Below his perch
red wings emerge to cruise above
the reeds among the dragon flies.

Between the banks a pair
of bulls feed from a winding
stream. Infrequently, they raise
their heads to shake away flies
or lift a leg, stretching haunch
or calf. They ignore muddy roots,
heat, birds, bugs, and honking horns
that claim parking spaces of their own.

These bulls will mark the equinox
by arching necks and slapping horns.
Blazing his fitness with his piss, one
stomps his hooves and rubs his horns
against the bark of trees. The other
lifts his head, swallows and exposes
his chest that is flecked with mud
in August dusk. Soon they will be
so consumed by the call, they'll risk
the softness of their flesh.

Locating the Pacific Crest Trail

Stopping my work before dark,
I come down a ridge and face
the sun. Beside me in rock
is a shelter, a stone seat.
Water carved a trough broken by
the roof's bush rooted ledge.
I know this is not a campsite
because the bench faces
directly into the sunset.
I leave my maps, canteens,
and bags on the trail.
I look towards the open clearing,
and there by its edge I see
the fine orange wings of a wasp,
large veins pulsing,
and the wasp releasing the spider.
It turns to check it
tapping the bug,
the ground with her tail.

Here in white oaks,
quail gather in front of a diamond-
back design drawn on an olla.*
Its color matches the hill's
barren site. I pick it up.
Inside is a pile of oak leaves,
a dozen acorns. I imagine
this jar in my living room
with sand up to its lip,
with a small barrel cactus
in front of three granite stones.
In the sunset hour known as the time

between the dog and coyote,
I know I can take the olla.
Know I am alone here,
can call what I find mine,
the sun west of Granite,
the moon rising, as one howl
lends to others its echoes.
Instead I load what I've brought
as dust appears in rays of sunlight,
on the dark green sides of leaves,
on fallen acorns, in eddies of wind,
which appear and die at the clearing's edge.

*An olla is a ceramic jar, often unglazed, used for cooking stews or soups, for the storage of water or dry foods.

The Gust of Wind

Spring rose clean as birches
during my last leap year home.
For the past ten years, I spent winter
afternoons on this lake. Soon I'd
be the first to graduate, but this evening
I skated with my hockey stick and some
primitive rhythm composed for blade
and tin. I shot the puck, an old tuna can,
away from the bridge's thin ice. Landing
on edge it rolled, skirting the shore's marshes.

My blades cut into ice, and speed
was skate-plowed snow dusting my feet.
Catching my puck, I drew a bead
on the pile of ice a fisherman made
to mark his site.

Slapping my stick against the ice, I whirled,
and my breathing followed the customs of its being.
I knew little about manhood coming as quick as spring,
or how to interpret these signs: chuckholes rimmed
with mud, icicles hung on Thunder Bridge;
a dog's nose tight to the ground on an island beach.

Maybe, they were designed to mean little
because nothing happened. The wind continued
to lie between winter and spring. As I skated,
I thought about how good it was that the islands —
like the ice — were full of cracking sounds.

Removing my cap, I raced the darkness.
On the bank I paused to catch my breath
before sprinting on the tips of my blades

to the basement. As I entered the house,
nothing could contain the joy of my youth;
except, the gust of wind, blowing mist
off the snow-capped fence.

Friday's Fish Supper

I remember the shade of the kitchen light,
my mother wearing a green sweater, John's
jean patch on his sleeve, my white sweat shirt,
and Dave wanted to fight for his right
to wear his red flannel undershirt.

Mike laughed as his teeth sliced
syllables of his speech.
Dan wiped tomato sauce
from his lips and cheeks.

He flipped a drop
right on impeccable Sue's blouse.
Mary bit the tip of her braid
and pulled her dress over her slip.
Folding her hands in her lap,
she looked at the light, rather
than let Sue know about the stain.
Dad, his tie pinned with a ruby clasp,
smiled, unaware of the game.

Finishing his pipe, he spoke
about the apostles being diligent.
We bowed our heads, said grace,
kept a moment of silence
as steam from the blue gill
became almost invisible.

The Soft Tug of the Tongue and Lips

When it snowed in January, the wooden
cupboards seemed part of a nursery rhyme.

She shoveled snow and salted the walk
to ease her anxiety during the sorting of bills.

At these times the soft tug of her nursing son's
tongue and lips made her want to cry. Then,

she pressed her ear against the curtains and counted
the number of times the blizzard shook the glass.

She watched snow sift through the screen
of evergreen and thinly coat the ground.

As the stirring child brought her in from the storm, she lifted
him from her breast and hummed 'Pea Soup and Johnny Cake.'

The snow continued to fall on the low growing pines.
Her rocker held its place beside her two-by-two window.

The baby smiled at her, and she rearranged
the boy in his blanket before urging him to feed.

Closing his eyes, he obeyed. Then, she turned her head
to watch the snow swirl above the shrubs.

Awakening

What we know
about the mockingbird
is next to nothing.

John says the bird mimics
everything it hears: a chainsaw,
a Jeep wrenching an iron post,
the squeaking of a wooden gate.

His wife says the bird mimics
only the animals it hears:
a feral cat, calling out its young,
and from her room, a woman
moaning in the early morning rain.

Ornithologists say that
a mockingbird mimics
other birds to confuse
birds of prey.

My wife says she doesn't care
what the mockingbird mimics
as long as it sings its song
somewhere far from us.

Perhaps, I respond, the mockingbird
was a raven in another life.
Having stolen the eggs
and the young of other birds,
it's condemned to sing songs
of the birds it terrorized and to fly
from tree to tree fleeing the bird it was.

This morning mist seemed trapped
between being fog or drizzle,
and I heard a mockingbird,
sobbing in the orange tree.

A Blizzard Drove

A blizzard drove through prairie fields
and blew under chapel doors.
The future knelt with those ordained
as winter settled on the Church.

Who could escape the snow and cold,
incense and Latin Chants? I would be
lying if I said I conjured memories of home
to calm my mind and enabled me to meditate.

During evening prayers I remember wishing
for a vision of Clear Lake, and the brothers
thumbing through hymn books reminded me
of the drum of wings from ducks engaging flight.

I remember longing to see the shallow hollow
where Cristina stood. Lifting tops of wooden hives,
she removed screens among the swarm of bees
that grouped above her blouse.

There was something about the winter wind.
When the chanting ended, the church became
deathly quiet for a moment. When a gust of wind
hit windows and doors, it startled me.

It was then I recalled her apiary, and how I walked
through my fear of bees in order to catch a glimpse
of her freckles that the breeze exposed
when it parted her curly bangs.

During a Family Reunion,

In a cabin built for a John Wayne western, I listened
to the wind blowing through the westerly window and
thought it foretold the arrival of another ordinary day.

Walking past the movie cabins, I hiked the Lake Shore Trail.
Nothing appeared in the westerly sky. Yet, I felt I'd been given
a gift of clean air as clouds passed over the woods.

Sitting on a log, I watched elk horns bob behind a trio
of shoulder-high pines. In an opening between the trees,
a doe and two fawns pointed their noses skyward.

Geese swam into a line as a woman, wading out, began to fish.
Was she using a Ginger Quill or a Brindle bug? I wondered,
peeling a branch to pry open the log. Ants rose beneath my stick.

Family stories about our Algonquin blood held no hints
of an inheritance of woods and water, nor should I expect
from my European side any birthright of steel and bricks.

Several types of fungus displayed autumn colors. Breaking one
from the log, I crumbled it between my palms. I felt that I
lost my ancestors' stories about visions or spirits.

Was their world reachable? I wondered as I watched the woman
fly fish. She casted, and casted, and one cast became a line falling
from sight before a trout pulled her rod downward.

She snapped her line, pulled the fish toward its tip
then swung the Rainbow in my direction. The sun flashed
off its scales as my shadow became one among shadows.

Landscape: Great Grandfather and Walnut Tree

Three maples line the north bank
of a stream named "the stream."
It divides his land between orchard
and wheat field. Kneeling,
he begins to weed the soil
behind the walnut's drip line.
As his hands smooth the soil,
he slides his leg closer to
the buried blade of his hoe.

If there's anything to find in the soil,
it's chips of wood, rocks, or the black
and cracked walnut husks.
He cocks his head to smell the creek waters
embedded in air. As the late sun exposes
the lines of his face,
he wipes tobacco spit from his chin.
Watching him kneel comfortably
in the Chapel of his life, I call his name
before I kneel beside him, pull weeds,
and crumble small clumps of soil.

The Afternoon of Good and Plenty

After the tombstones saluted,
I saw forgiveness for those
who had courage
to land at Normandy
but not to march in Selma,

who had the courage to protest the war
but not to accept the soldier,
to bury the dead
but not to kiss the corpse.

After the flag-wrapped coffins
blossomed brutally in sunlight,
I saw forgiveness for those
who had courage
to arrest the criminal
but not to resist the lynch mob.

After the tulips' clench-fisted
salute, I saw forgiveness for those
who had courage to pray
but not to swallow their own slurs,
relaxing in the shade
beneath their tongues,

who had the courage to look
into rusty mirrors
of ancient manuscripts
but not to discount the ageless
theories of cultural nationalism.

Now in the afternoon of good and plenty
the corpse of my life arrives.
Who will forgive the chairs
for being too soft, the air too fresh,
the plums too plump?

Who will forgive the writer
for writing but not speaking,
for failing to become
a brother to the shell- shocked,
for imaging that he would kiss
the corpse if the rain
waited a minute more?

Blue Stool

this room begins
behind the mushroom
colored door
with its two dead bolts
and dry rot jamb

with its bird droppings
on the window sill among
the Wheaties crumbs
and the forked-claw prints

dressing in the curtain's
shadow a man buckles
his belt he could be
a retired CEO down
on his luck

he could be a homeless man
rescued from the street but
he isn't he is a man
who live in an upstairs
apartment downtown

month after month
he lives here with
these half-spread wings
these yellow beaks
a few coos

and centuries
of wheat fields
in the bowl
he placed
on the blue stool

Kings River Canyon

This old, bald pine has to know its dying.
Maybe it overheard the whispers
of evergreens, growing on these
glacier-sheered cliffs, or maybe
the pine knows it intuitively
as it knows yearly it has to manage
to squeeze out a thin ring
between heart and bark.

Only in the middle does this
old tree show any green.
The top ten feet are marked
entirely by dead branches.
In the lower twenty feet,
bees nest in a charcoal scar
from an old fire.

They form a blossom, brushing
back a ribbon of sunshine
that threads itself through
shade and ground fog.
At its base squirrels abandon
old tunnels to dig new ones. Yet,
this tree still roots down in the face
of winter, in the face of a spring thaw.

In the grip of summer's
morning breeze, it creaks
as it stands solitary and cinctured
by a semi-circle of saplings
too supple to creak.

Meditation on An Uplifted Beach

I

Through brush, grass, dirt
come steel tracks
and rubber tires.
They uncover bones
of dolphins, whales, birds.
Sometimes thin rust lines
outline their graves,
always their heads higher
than their tails.

I hold these dolphin bones.
Three vertebras
survived
excavation.
At this hour
a rabbit's ear
rubs buckwheat branches.
The quick crow shadow
glides,
and I think
of the dolphin's last days.

Fearful of drowning
it swims towards shore.
Weakening in the surf, it beaches.
Soon sea birds eat strips
of dolphin meat,
as salt hardens around the blow hole,
as the tide leaves pools in its wounds,
as its dreams fill with bird calls,
waves, and the fog weaves a light cool fabric.

II

I learned to quietly stand,
feeling the weight of my tool bags.
What is there for me to understand
about the size, make,
age of my tools?
Hand level,
black and brass, it shines through use
not polish.
A plumb bob's
chipped point touches the hub,
connecting me to all the site's coordinates.
I run my eye
along the notched edge
of my adz.
These are my parts
waiting to be buried
in a landfill after my death.
Will my hand bones remember
this flesh grown thick with use,
this finger flattened under a ripper tooth,
another hammer-scarred?
Will they remember
holding this rock bone?
It is the size and shape of a miniature rose.
It fractures
and its grains stream like sand.

III

I look at one bone.
It is brown
with a sand dollar pattern.
Feldspar grains
sparkle along ridges.

This bone sensed sun's heat,
water's heat,
heat of the hunt
as this dolphin
dove through a school.
Fish, blood, kelp leaves
milled together
in a dense water wall
out of this a shark appears
like winter storms
when water whipped
as flashes of metal
across its skin.
It appears
with a raw double row of teeth
in a head
with eyes rolled back.
This vision drove the dolphin to high leaps.
Forced it to walk backwards on its tail,
as it screamed and pumped
its front flippers.
My eyes walk
along scars
on my hands, arms.
Walk along narrow scars
on my hammers handle.
Walk along pocked scars
on my hammers head.
In this bone
are silted holes
from percolating water.
They tell me
in the end
there is no promise
the earth
will be kind.

IV

I hold this bone-sand crescent
above the water,
above rip tides,
moon tides,
tides of the equinox.
I think how at times
the dolphin watched the sun set,
as I watch the sun set.
In the distance
it is white heat,
white light,
and now
the rim of the horizon
marked
star by star.

Yellowstone Meditation #4
Sunday School

As a second grader, I wanted prayer to be based
on faith and for it to behave like Noah's dove

which God eventually gave a twig
in answer to Noah's petition.

As a man it is as hard to believe Noah's story as it is
to believe our souls change into fish to enter the afterlife.

Perhaps, this is why my prayers seem to scratch
for seeds in the grass between the seedlings.

Maybe, that's why it's easy to forget the night prayers
as I watch water drain through the grainy soil.

When the geyser blows, her streams of boiling
liquid build a mound of pebbles.

The nun said pray correctly and as God sent
Noah a twig, He would send us wisdom.

As I listen to the ranger talk about the Blackfoot,
I remember the nun's thin rimmed glasses.

The ranger said the tribes using Yellowstone cooked
their fish in these boiling pools. The tribe believed the fish

came willingly to the eater. The eater thanked the gods
for their gift before becoming a gift of food for lesser game.

Bell Ringer

Sweeping the coffee shop
a girl smiles
remembering a joke
we all know,
or a party at the cove,
or a close-cropped boy.

As she sidesteps her pile of dust,
the bells sown to the cuffs
of her mid-calf trousers ring
as delicately as the hairs curl
around the corner of her eye.

In a few years
who will remember
this moment of beauty?

If someone would
present her with a fig,
it would be pornographic.

If someone would present her
with an apple, it would be
a failure of feeling.

Landscape of a Young Woman and a Pool

A stream flows through a triangle of scrub oak
and drops over a ledge into a pool. Along the bank
yuccas bloom between mountain lilacs.

She sits on a rock, dipping her feet
into the pool; then, she slides into
the water as if slipping into a garment.

How happy she seems as she bounces
until the water line encompasses her hips.
When oak shade falls evenly upon her shoulders,

she decides to return to the granite slab. As she
steps onto the rocks, the water runs down her legs
into the pool like threads returning to the loom.

Taking a deep breath, she jumps.
Surfacing, she swims and dives, appearing
and disappearing like an apparition.

Below the Feet of Orion — Huanusco, Mexico

I

During the summer solstice, the moon light hit the waves,
breaking against stones that the river placed
perpendicular to the current. Villagers used them
as a bridge from their homes to their church.
On the night before Felipa's funeral, they carried her body
across these flat rocks for the viewing and saying of the rosary.

Twisting the leaves with its cold hands, the wind acted like
it was autumn. Parishioners behaved as if the wind's actions
marked the night with an evil eye. No one dared to look
at the cross in the graveyard. Woman wrapped their shawls
tightly around their throats. Men turned up the collars
of their shirt and gripped their hats. The frogs ceased croaking.

Mosquitos disappeared beneath the cottonwood canopy.
The crickets set aside their fiddles as silence became
visible like river fog, settling on the cobble streets.
After the funeral of my wife's great-aunt, Patsy
returned with Felipa's picture. It was taken in '41
when her aunt was a young woman.

Felipa sat beside her husband in a restaurant.
She had turned away from him and focused
on her wedding ring. She was not angry; although,
he told her he would go north. He would work in the fields.
The war was on. There was plenty of work. He would send
for her. They would make a new life.

As if she fought against frowning, her lips sagged.
Forgetting to knock the ash off her cigarette, she squinted
as she sat with her wine beside her husband. He looked

at the table's distant corner. The bill of his wool cap
shadowed his forehead. He forgot to unbutton his coat
and sat with his hands pushed deep into his coats pockets.

He would hop the freight. He would pick crops. His decision
showed itself by the way his clenched jaw bulged at the joint.
If Felipa saw into the future, she might have seen her man
stacking crates four high. He walked from south of Calexico
with glowing blisters. He learned from his weight,
his cramping thighs, and the duff rolled in his palms.

Did he envision this scene? When the farm truck parked,
workers hung shirts on plank siding. The odor of black sage
brought downslope the smell of a woman. It reminded him
of Felipa's hands damp from laundry. Her man, a thin man,
fisted his ring hand in his pocket. He watched five crows
chase a hawk. He rubbed his fingers across his nose and mouth.

Could she see him building a tent of tumbleweeds in a triangle
of ocotillos? If she saw anything, Felipa saw dust and sky outside
the window. She did not know he'd wrap his cotton shirt around
his head, nor could she see him turn over a beehive, or a rancher,
pull two hundred stingers from his back, hire him, pay him a few
dollars an hour his first year and give him a raise his second.

She couldn't imagine his boss teaching him to lift screens,
gather honey, and work among hives without fearing the bees
who entered his dreams as quills of light. She knew about
the six men pulled from their wreckage. One man's shoe
left in chemise, another's face pinned with bone slivers, a thread
of blood on his neck. Six men carried up a slope, placed in a line.

Maybe she saw his death at a railway crossing, or
her fear that circled the room like cigarette smoke.
As I held the picture, my wife spoke, and her voice became

soft like waves lapping the sides of rocks, and her eyes held broad
leaf shadows that were thick with woody underbrush. When she
touched me, her hand … opened like the bud of a psalm of sorrow.

II

Two years before Felipa's death my wife and I visited her.
As we entered her village, the cobble paving seemed older
than the river. Near the rear of the church, the lone
gas pump appeared as lonely as the statue of St. Francis,
which birds spotted with their droppings and feathers.

Fifty years ago, her husband died, and she became the old woman,
found in many villages in Mexico. She became the teacher.
She became the baby sitter. Her nose became enormous and
distinguished her from the other old woman in the village.
Don't laugh.

She wore her enormous nose like a mark of distinction.
On the end of her nose grew a wart with two hairs
sprouting out of it. These hairs remained constantly
in one's vision. Lower your eyes and their shadow seemed
to cross your feet. She lived. The wart lived. The hairs lived.

Beneath her chin, a growth pulsed like a sock
filled with worms. When she strung red peppers,
it radiated heat. When she talked, she held it,
and it shaded her voice with the color of rain.
Don't laugh.

The neighbors who saw her return from the mill
labeled her a witch or a saint. Could it be the fault
of the morning fog's for enclosing her and making
her seem beyond time? Wrapped in her shawl,
she carried her bucket of corn.

Mothers sent their small children to learn from her.
They bought candy from her. In return she told them
their history. The older children mocked her to hide
their fear that her age and face might conceal a witch
or a saint. Still, she told them stories:

> This is your grandfather's hole.
> He dug it with his finger while he courted your grandmother.
> To control his nerves, he whittled with his pen knife
> a hole in the mortar. In those days
> young men only saw women in doorways
> or through windows.
> Finished with his day's work, he would stop
> with sugar cane tied in bundles
> to the back of his horse.
> In the door of this house
> he spoke until your grandmother
> had to help with dinner.
> Early in the morning, he led his horse pass this house
> your grandmother waited for him. They walked together.
> She carried her bucket of grain to the mill.
> At the fork he went left. She went right. I watched them.

After our introduction, Felipa gave me a small plastic statue
of Christ. Her son said, "Don't lose it. Place it
where others can see. Be sure to tell the story of how you
came to own it. Tell the story with respect, don't profane
her memory." Later on the way to the store, he said,

"She may be a witch or a saint?
Esta es muy importante,"
He wanted to tell me more as we walked
the cobble trail, which is a narrow street
in Huanusco, but a mocking bird dove at him.

We stopped at Juanita's grocery store.
We bought four bottles of beer, three bottles of Seven Up.
We returned to Felipa's home. She cooked over a wood fire.
The shadows of flame lit up the growth on her neck.
It seemed to pulse as she talked to herself.

Embarrassed at being caught in conversation
with herself, she said to me, "I am so old
with no one to talk to except the cockroaches
and flies. I talk to myself because I am afraid
I will forget how to speak."

While waiting for my wife to arrive with corn
from the mill, Felipa shared with us peanuts,
grown by the river. They were not roasted.
They were not salted. They were green and
kept in a feed sack.

As I snacked, her face told stories. The size of her nose
related the weight of sorrow that death left her village.
Her wrinkles appeared like scars, outlining the bulges
of her cheeks. When she pulled her hair into a bun,
her cheeks became a map of desert graves.

When my wife arrived, Felipa became happy, and the fire
leaped and licked. As she began to cook, the kindness
in her heart expressed itself in the color of her sauce as well
as in the crispness of her tortillas. After dinner she poured cups
of tea and soda. We sat outside where she began her story.

> On Sunday afternoons, eight girls played
> on the banks of the village river.
> They wore rainbow colored dresses.
> Their braids contained many ribbons.

> Every Sunday they played by the river.
> One night they would not stop playing.
> Their parents called them.
> Her friends and Felipa refused to leave.
> They danced in a circle.
> Their parents called them.
> They held hands in the circle.
> The river became angry
> and slapped its waves on top
> of the flat rock bridge.
>
> It was Poncha's fault.
> She would not let them leave.
> Finally, Felipa could no longer
> resist her mother's call
> for she was only a young girl,
> a good girl.
> She wanted to play with her friends.
> She wanted to go home to her mother.
> Felipa wanted to dance.
> She wanted to eat.
> She pleaded with Poncha.
> She pleaded with her friends.
> No one listened.
> She became mad like the river.
> She fell down, skinned her elbow.

Felipa paused to point to her scar.

> She left her friends
> who danced and laughed
> as she ran up the path
> to the village.

She points to the spot where the cobblestone begins.

It was at that precise
location that she heard
the river yell and turned
towards her friends.
It was then she saw them
rise in the air.

Felipa will never forget it.

They rose as they danced in a circle.
They rose, spinning into the evening sky.

This is true she said and points to them in the sky.
She identifies them below the feet of Orion.
I know those stars as the Pleiades.
She knows them as Poncha,
     Sonia,
          Andrea,
              Tonia,
                  Dora,
                       Juanita,
                            and
                                Guillermena.

Author Biography

Joseph Milosch graduated in 1995 with his MFA from San Diego State University. He has published poetry and essays in various magazines, and has had multiple nominations for the Pushcart Award. His first book *The Lost Pilgrimage Poems* was published by Poetic Matrix Press.

He received an honorable mention for his poetry in The Chapel Jazz Poetry Contest in the spring of 1999.

He received an Excellence in Literature award from Mira Costa College.

His first chapbook, *On the Wing*, was published by Barnes and Noble as a regional publication, and his second chapbook, *Father of Boards and Woodwinds*, was published by the Inevitable Press for the Laguna Poets Series. He was a finalist in the Tennessee Middle State Chapbook contest in 1996 for his chapbook, *If I Could Imagine*. He won the 1997 Tennessee Middle State Chapbook contest with his chapbook *Among Men*. In 1999 The Laguna Poets Series published his fourth chapbook *Now She Bends Away* with Inevitable Press.

Press Producers

Friend of the Press
– Heartfelt Thanks

Anatoly Molotkov
Beverly Riverwood
Lilith Rogers
S. Preston Chase
Joan Michelson
Anonymous

Supporter of the Press
– Deepest Gratitude

Judith Tucker
Linda Milks
Rebecca Hubbard
Magick
Diana Badger
Miles Peterson
Susan Dullack
Mary Eisenhauer
Lillian Madera Schuller
Michael Milosch
Zachary Ritter
Maria Rosales
Patricia Kelly
Jean Wong
Linda McGonigal
Katelin Holloway &
Ben Ramirez
Anonymous

Sponsor of the Press
– Profound Appreciation

J. Glenn & Barbara Evans
Joyce Downs
Nicole Woo
Sylvia Levinson
Tricia Ferguson
Edward Maupin
Clare & Jon Allen
Sharon Bard
Kelly Gazaway
Cynthia Albers
Ailbe O'Brien
Anonymous

Patron of the Press
– Keen Affection

Paul Dolinsky
Tomas Gayton
Carina Wagner
Peggy Gregory
Albert G. Jordan
Sandra Stillwell
Chris Hoffman
Joseph Milosch
The Entrekin Foundation
Anonymous

Press Producers

I would like to thank all of those who worked on and participated in our *Summer 2013 Season of Poetry* campaign to raise finances for this and two other volumes of poetry. Thanks to James Downs, Devon Peterson, Joyce Downs, and Dan Davis. Also, thanks to the three poets; Lyn Lifshin, Raphael Block and Joseph Milosch. And of course all of these people who contributed so generously to this effort. Small poetry press publishing is a joy to do but certainly cost money and these Producers, like in any artistic effort, are the ones who make it possible.

Thank you!

—John Peterson, Publisher

www.ingramcontent.com/pod-product-compliance
Lightning Source LLC
Chambersburg PA
CBHW021022090426
42738CB00007B/869